Good For You

Good For You

114 Mindful Practices Every Woman Can Adopt
For A More Harmonious Life

Stacy-Ann Buchanan

Good For You
114 Mindful Practices Every Woman Can Adopt
For A More Harmonious Life

Copyright © 2023 by Stacy-Ann Buchanan

All rights reserved.

This book or any portion thereof may not be reproduced by any electronic or mechanical means, including information storage and retrieval systems, without written permission from the author except for the use of brief quotations in a book review.

If you would like permission to use material from the book (other than for review purposes), please contact info@stacyannbuchanan.com.

Thank you for your support.

ISBN
Ebook ISBN 978-1-7387798-2-6
Paperback ISBN 978-1-7387798-0-2
Hardcover ISBN 978-1-7387798-1-9

Cover design by Kamar Martin

but God.

For my daughter

Dearest Frantz,

For almost a decade, you were my most prayed-prayer, my most wished-wish and my most desired-dream.

Everyday I thank God for his greatest gift to me—you!
You are my joy. You are my light. And. You are my anchored why.
Being your mother is my highest honour. Loving you is my greatest desire.
You are everything, Frantz—my everything.

Everytime I look at you, I see - love, faith, miracle, dream and joy—personified. You have taught me the true essence of being a cheerleader and an encourager. And. I'm deeply honoured and truly blessed that you have chosen me to be your guide, your protector, your nurturer, and your mommy as you embark on your mission in this lifetime.

This book was birthed because of you.
This book is for you.
It's for the yesterday-you, the today-you, and the tomorrow-you.

I love you my sunshine, my li'l revolutionary.

Thank you for choosing me.

Love you forever,
Mommy

p.s. - whenever life gives you the choice to sit it out or dance....I hope you always choose to dance.

To Carla

Good For You

Carla,

You are arguably my soulmate. Point blank. Period. I have never met another human being to whom I am so divinely connected to. When you yin, I yang and when I yang, you yin. The combination of our Leo + Gemini energies blaze perfectly together and our relationship epitomizes magic.

*I remember this moment distinctively - when I filed for my divorce a few years back, I told no-one. I figured it was a decision I had to make alone. After the fact though, you were the first friend I called to share the news with. Upon telling you, your first words to me were, "**Good for you**!" I paused 'cause in my head, I was wondering why you'd find my 'failure'— good? You picked up on my pause and you quickly followed with, "I say, good for you, Stacy, because I am sick and tired of the narrative that paints women as a failure after a divorce! This took a lot of guts, and I'm so proud of you! Just so you know, you haven't failed—this is your brand-new beginning and I'll be here to cheer you on! So, Good. For. Fucking. You!"*

That comment—that response—that support; they changed my outlook on my situation and were just what my soul needed at the time.

The phrase, "good for you" is the catchphrase of our friendship, and not one conversation between us goes without us saying it. We use this as the badge to honour our friendship because we both strongly believe that in life, when things happen—whether they're good or bad—the underlying outcome is always for you and never to you. And when it's for you, it's always good.

So thank you, Carla. And good for us! Good for us for having each other, good for us for celebrating this magical friendship, and good for us living our most authentic lives!

Additionally, there are many other loved ones I want to thank for making this book.

To my ancestors - Thank you for walking so that I can run. I aspire to continue to be your wildest dreams.

To my parents—Kenneth and Janet—Mommy and Daddy. Thank you for being my support system, my nurturers, my guides, prayer warriors, my providers, and for loving me unconditionally. The wisdom you've imparted unto me throughout these years has nourished me into the woman I am today. I am forever grateful. I love you both. Eternally.

To my immediate family, my roots, my extended family and my friends (too many to single-handedly name). Thank you for your love, your support, your encouragement, your prayers, and your nourishment. I love and appreciate you all and am forever grateful to have you as an integral part of my growth and as my cheering squad. That type of love and support can never be replaced, nor replicated. I am in awe. I'm appreciative. I am honoured. Many thanks.

To Aunty Sheila —thank you. Your belief in me, your love for me, your continuous encouragement, and your prayers are eternally appreciated. I love you.

To Juju—you are the most courageous young woman I know. You are a force, you are a vibe, and more importantly, you are—you. I am grateful for your love, I am delightfully engulfed by your stories, and I am appreciative for the lens I've gained in watching you grow and step into your greatness. I love you, and I am so proud of you.

Good For You

In community.

To my supporters—my community. Thank you for believing in me. Thank you for celebrating with me. Thank you for rooting for me. Thank you for supporting me. Thank you for your encouragement over the years. I appreciate y'all.

Contents

Dear Woman (prelude)	xxv
Chapter One	**1**
Your Emotional Health Matters	3
Chapter Two	**25**
Your Mental Health Matters	27
Chapter Three	**57**
Your Spiritual Health Matters	59
Chapter Four	**85**
Your Physical Health Matters	87
Chapter Five	**107**
You Matter	109
Dear _____ (add your name here)	
Letter to Future Self (conclusion)	139

Good For You

Dear Woman,

May you understand that every chapter of your life is written by you and only you.
May you stop allowing others to impose their narrative upon your life.
May you assertively fire and hire according to your needs.
May you be the director and producer of your life.

May you reclaim your divine feminine power.

May you focus on your healing and your well-being.
May you go through it, grow from it, and then glow.
May you recognize your self-worth, add your taxes, and charge them insurance.
May you cut any relationship umbilical cord that makes you feel inadequate.
May you be in spaces where you are celebrated and not tolerated.

May you distance yourself from anyone who tampers with your mental and emotional health.

May you appreciate your unique beauty.
May you drink your water, mind your business, and do your squats.
May you find ways to always nourish your being.
May you take up space.
May you indulge in guilt-free rests.

May you be reminded of your softness and your healing powers.

May you lift others while you climb.
May celebrate your wins and the wins of other women.
May you know the power of your voice.
May you hone into the pillar of strength that is rooted within you.

More importantly, may you know that - you are enough.

Love to you,

Stacy-Ann Buchanan

Good For You

may these mindful practices bring forth a magical lens in which you can view the beauty of your world.

Chapter One

may your connections be fruitful, nurturing, and transformative.

Your Emotional Health Matters

Someone once said to me, "The whole world sees you as motivating and inspiring, but you're nothing but trash."
I cried.
While I was crying, the person then said, "Are you gonna go back to being depressed? This time you should kill yourself!"

Those words sent an avalanche of emotions that echoed throughout my entire body. At that very moment I realized that I no longer wanted this choice and that this emotional labour I have been subconsciously harbouring was slowly eating away at my intelligence.

One major lesson I've learned on my journey of self-love, self-care and self-appreciation is this: you are the author of your life. The choices you make today are the blueprint for your future.

Choose wisely.

xoxo

You can be hurting and healing at the same time. And that's okay. The key is to never get so comfortable in your pain that you forget your happiness is still an option.

Healing is mucky. Healing is dirty. Healing is painful. It sometimes requires isolation, and it hurts; however, it's also the most liberating, freeing and rewarding thing you could ever do for yourself. When you sum it all up, healing does not mean that the damage was never done. It means that you no longer allow it to control your life.

Healing is never linear and healing doesn't happen overnight. In order for you to heal, you must address the emotions that transpired from your pain. And, in order for you to heal, you must first feel. Do the work and trust your healing process.   Your future self will thank you.

The pain and trauma you're going through may not be your fault, but the healing is 100% your responsibility. So gift yourself the permission to cut ties with your past and move forward with your healing. You owe your future self that.

It's not the job of others to start your healing journey for you and mistreating anyone while you process your pain won't stop your wound. You'll only end up delaying your own healing while subsequently shutting out those who care for you.

Do yourself a favour and don't stay updated with those who you realized weren't good for you. You honestly don't need to know how they're doing. And while you're at it, cut the social media umbilical cord as well—especially if checking up on them brings misery to your life and disturbs your peace.

Close that chapter of your story and walk confidently into your new beginning.

Stop trying to keep people around who do not want to be kept. Let them go.

You'll only continue to block your own blessings by trying to hold on to what God has removed. You have two choices: continue to re-read that chapter, or close that chapter and start writing the next.

Stop giving people who refuse to grow and who are hellbent on hurting you, a revolving door access to your life. Remember: when people show you who they are, believe them.

Forgiving them does not require reconnecting with them.

There are some people that should be loved from afar, especially if having them in your life brings you more pain than joy.

Is forgiveness necessary? Sure! But forgiveness is for you (your mental and emotional growth) not for the forgiven.

Develop an intimate relationship with your body. Get to know both your body and mind so well that you can establish the difference between guidance from your intuition versus that stemming from your traumas, which may mislead you.

'What if' statements are a disservice to yourself. They interfere with your happiness and block the flow of the present moment.

There are two things in life that you cannot control: what people say about you and what people think about you. You can only control your reaction. And your reaction should always be—**don't** take it personal.

The most important relationship you'll ever have in your entire existence is the relationship with yourself—period! And that relationship should be one that is healthy and thriving, rather than toxic and abusive. So be gentle with yourself—you are your greatest asset.

In order to love who you are, you can't hate the experiences that shape you.

And. The most powerful thing that a woman can do is own her story.

It equates to loving yourself, paving your journey in this lifetime, being aware of your self-worth, and unapologetically going for everything you want.

It happened not to you, but for you.

Every bit of your story creates a version of you that didn't exist before.

So, you can either let your story define you or let it refine you. The choice is yours!

Remember; any time God takes something from you, he always—always—replaces it with an upgrade!

Boundaries are a form of self-care. Block, mute, unfollow and unfriend are also forms of self-care. At all costs, protect your space and protect your peace.

If your friends can cry with you, they should be able to cheer for you too. If not, re-evaluate that friendship.

It's so easy to get caught up in the world of 'closure.'

It's so easy to believe that people need to give you a reason as to why they deserted their relationship with you; furthermore, it's so easy to believe the closure will set you free.

Honestly, the need for closure is not a necessity.

You see, having the need, and waiting for closure only sets you back in your life and prevents you from growing. And what does growth do? It makes you glow! Why would you want to stunt your growth and dim your own light? Take ownership of your own narrative by neither relying on getting nor giving closure to relationships or situations that wreaked havoc on your peace.

Chapter Two

may you always remember to be grateful for what you have.

Your Mental Health Matters

A few years ago, I realized that I was running on High Functioning Anxiety.

Hard work, non stop grind, securing bags, networking queen, and being booked and busy were all hats that I proudly wore.

You couldn't tell me nothin' and you couldn't get me to slow me down.

My posts would humbly share my accolades, but beneath it all laid an ego that constantly needed to be stroked—needed to be reminded that I'm that B!

Publicly, I was winning.
Privately, I was in a tug-o-war with my anxiety.

It wasn't until I began my healing journey that I realized that those years, where my career was highlighted, and where I spent my days basking in the glorified spotlight and working nonstop, were actually signs of High Functioning Anxiety.

Surprisingly, this seemed to be my norm, but when I broke it down and became self-aware of my habits, it was easy to identify the following traits:

1. What the public viewed as hardworking was my fear of failure.
2. What you saw as active was my inability to slow down.
3. What people saw as outgoing - was my fear of missing out and people-pleasing.
4. My loyalty—the one I dubbed as me being a 'Loyal Leo'—basically equated to my having poor boundaries.
5. What you saw as super-supportive - was me having trouble saying no. And,
6. What the public viewed as detailed-orientated —something always present at my events—was really my chronic overthinking

Please learn from me.

Good For You

Be mindfully aware of subscribing to 'hustle culture.' It's toxic; it's a blatant assault on your mental health; it's a total disregard of your well-being as it glamourizes unhealthy lifestyles and romanticizes workaholism and productivity, which are simply unsustainable. And for what? At the cost of one's well-being?

Let me get deeply personal right now....

As my curiosity, my need to connect to my ancestors, and as my work as a Mental Health Advocate dives deeper into intergenerational trauma, I realize that the hustle mentality has been forced onto my enslaved ancestors as a means of being productive.

That very same colonial mindset has been hustled down (pun intended) throughout generations. We've then adopted that mindset as a way of being productive and feeling worthy to counteract being called lazy—a term that has been used to shame us for centuries while actively promoting capitalism, white supremacy, and oppression. In reality, it's mentally and emotionally destructive.

In the process of decolonizing my mind, I have unsubscribed from the 'hustle culture' and subscribed to the 'alignment culture.'
I muted/unfollowed any accounts on social media that push the "hustle culture" agenda.
I no longer work hard—I work smart.
I stand firm in my affirmation that I no longer have to chase anything, 'cause what's meant for me will never miss me.

Finally, I no longer feel guilty for resting—I honour my ancestors by doing so. They have done enough.

You may get a rush of adrenaline or feel a sense of accomplishment from hustling, but please know that all the accolades, and all the $$$ in the world means nothing if you don't have your health to enjoy it.

xoxo

Your mental illness does not define you.

'You look happier', is the best compliment you can receive.

Therapy and Jesus can be in the same sentence.
Therapy and gym can be in the same sentence.
Therapy and meditation can be in the same sentence.
Stop ostracizing therapy.
Stop being ashamed of therapy.
Normalize therapy.
Therapy is one of the main components to your healing journey.
Therapy is the best investment you can make in yourself.

Sometimes peace is better than being right 'cause in the long run, protecting your mental health is better than jading your karma.

Unlearning requires patience. Relearning requires trial and error. And that's okay. You are a beautiful work in progress.

Mixed signals are confusing—God never ever sends confusion. So for the sake of your well-being—your mental health and your peace—take mixed signals as a big NO and move on with your life.

A safe space isn't necessarily a physical place—a safe space starts within you. Create it.

Don't answer your phone if you don't want to talk.

Reply to texts and emails at your convenience (not the earliest convenience for others).

Learn to say no without an explanation.

Leave events, conversations and interactions when you feel drained.

Your anxiety constantly lies to you. You are beautiful. You are amazing. You are enough.

Don't force yourself to be positive all the time. Give yourself the permission to feel your emotions. Your feelings are valid.

Say goodbye to people and things in your life that tamper with your mental health.

If you continue to pour from an empty cup, you'll end up depleting yourself until there's nothing left to give.

Get rid of that mindset that 'struggle' deserves a badge of honour. It doesn't. You should never put yourself in that position.

Your value isn't defined by how much pain you can endure, but instead by what you choose to put down and walk away from.

Putting yourself first is not selfish. It's selfless. When you do so, you'll be of more value to yourself and to your loved ones.

As you evolve, you'll never again invite or choose to entertain anyone who defies your boundaries.

Let me let you in on a li'l secret.
Peace isn't boring.
Peace means you can focus.
Peace means you can create your own happiness.
And.
Peace contributes to freedom from stress, anxieties, and worries.
Stay away from anyone who is determined to bring toxic drama to your life to 'spice it up.'
Peace is enough spice.

Narcissist.

nar.cis.sist /ˈnärsəsəst/

noun

a person who has an excessive interest in or admiration of themselves.

A narcissist can wreak havoc on your mental health. They have this li'l game that they like to play called, "Imma cut you off just so that you can feel pain and come running back to me or beg me to talk to you."
They are the biggest and trickiest manipulators that you'll ever meet.
Here are four ways to beat a narcissist at their own game:
1. Don't fall for their gaslighting and manipulation.
2. Instead of arguing when they start in on you, flip the script and walk away.
3. Refuse to let their behaviour affect you. Choose peace.
4. Remember: you don't beat a narcissist by trying to let them see their disorder, by loving them more or by giving them your attention. You beat a Narcissist at their own game by taking away their life supply—your attention.

Words are powerful. Be mindful of the words you utter to yourself. What comes out of your mouth comes into your life. Use them selectively, especially when speaking of and to yourself.

Be mindful of who and what you choose to follow on social media. Afterall, your feed eventually feeds your mind.

Say no to 'stress money.' No amount of dollar$ and exposure is worth disturbing your spiritual health, confusing your emotional health, and tampering with your mental health. Say no to being booked and busy and yes to being paid and peaceful.

Do not compare yourself and your journey with anyone. We all walk different paths in life and at different paces. Rest assured that what's meant for you will never, ever miss you.

People's opinions of you—whether good or bad—should never alter how you feel about yourself. You're the only one who can—and who should—determine your own worth.

Check on yourself regularly and check yourself regularly.

Chapter Three

may you always honour your intuition.

Your Spiritual Health Matters

One thing I've had to adapt in my life is the freedom that comes with letting go and letting God.

I've spent a majority of my life holding on to things and people that I should've let go a long time ago; in doing so, I ended up causing my own storm and prolonging a mere chapter into two or three chapters.

And then, I ended up letting those chapters define my life.

How dare I? How dare I serve myself with such injustice and mindful lies?

As I got older and subsequently wiser, I've adopted one main mandate that has since provided me with an abundance of peace: if it comes, let it, and if it goes, let it.

Yes—I've had some pretty tough chapters in my life, but that's all they were—chapters.

And those chapters didn't define me, they refined me.

So, today I want you to trust the process and timing of your life and just breathe.

This is just a chapter, love. Not your whole story.

xoxo

*Your intuition is your spirit guide.
Trust your intuition.
Put some respect on your intuition.
Afterall, she is never wrong.*

When God makes you wait for something, it's not his way of depriving you, but rather his means of changing you. To get what you have asked for, he has to prepare you for it. Everything you desire is coming. Keep the faith.

In order to glow, you must first go through it—then grow from it.

If you can dream it, if you can think it, if you can imagine it, if you can see it—then it's already yours and it does exist.

Whenever someone decides to exit your life, take it as a sign that that chapter has closed and where God is taking you—that person's presence will serve no purpose and or hold you back.

Please stop sleeping on yourself.
Please stop waiting for Tom, Dick, Harry, Suzette or Babara to give you that big break.
If you don't see your name on a door, build one.
Be the change that you want to see.
And know that if God gives you the vision, he will always provide you with the people and tools necessary to execute it.

Replace worrying with prayer—let your faith be the down payment for your future.

Some people may 'love you' but they just don't want you to be doing better than them. You'll know this, because while you're always speaking life into them, they—on the other hand—are always trying to unplug your lamp.

Always go where you're celebrated, not where you are tolerated.

A lot of times you're not invited because they fear you will steal the attention.

Sometimes you're not tagged or mentioned because they don't want others to know who you are and what you do.

and....Oftentimes they'll purposely close the door on you and tell you that you're not ready or that there isn't a place for you at the table because they feel threatened by your light and influence.

Don't let them stop you. Keep being you—acknowledge your greatness and shine your brightest. Your existence is a divine purpose.

Whenever life presents you with two options and you don't know which one to choose, always pick the one that will let you sleep better at night. That's the choice that will bring you peace. Peace is the blueprint for success.

Trust your waiting period—that's where the magic happens.

Sometimes we don't realize the blessings we have until we no longer have them. Appreciate everything you have in your life and take nothing for granted.

Remember: being blessed is a condition of the heart and a frame of mind.

A reminder:

Your dreams are not too small.
Your desires are not too small.
Your goals are not too small.
But—
You gotta trust the process.
You gotta walk by faith and never by sight.
And more importantly,
You gotta understand that things don't happen on your time—they happen on God's divine timing. Trust the process.

Living your most authentic life is knowing and walking in your purpose. When you do so - you own your narrative, keep your power, and maintain your peace.

Learn to trust the timing of your life. Learn to trust that your dreams/goals are actually footsteps for what God has in store for you. And more importantly, if God blocked it, don't stalk it.

Being aware of your choices and living your life without other people's validation creates confidence, which is definitely when your best life begins and will continue until eventually every single area of your life is filled with nothing but the purest love!

Never feel inclined or pressured to share your whole story. Not every chapter of your story needs to be read out loud. Remember, you have the utmost control over which chapter(s) of your life you choose to read out loud and which ones you choose to keep to yourself.

Sometimes you'll meet someone for the first time and—instinctively and intuitively—know that you want to spend your life with or without them. (read this again). Honour that.

Sometimes a 'great opportunity' is really a great opportunist in disguise. To filter between the two, always put God before and in the midst of every decision that you make. Also, keep in mind that closed doors do not mean you've been rejected. It simply means that God is redirecting you to something bigger and better!

Some people will approach you with the sweetest most flattering words, yet their inner core—their energy—just oozes hate, jealousy, and bad-mind. If you ever sense that in another person, run. See, the thing is that people lie, but energy does not! And if you're at the stage where you're not spiritually aware and cannot differentiate between the two, then pray and ask God for clarity.

Here's a friendly reminder. Saying no should not equate to you being a 'horrible person'. Saying no simply means you know your worth—you know your mental, emotional, and physical capacity, you respect yourself, and most importantly, saying no means you are spiritually aligned with energies. 'No' takes courage. Be courageous.

When you're close to your goals, you get the most obstacles thrown your way. You have to understand that the enemy listens to your prayers as well, and when he sees that you're about to get your blessings, he throws everything in your path to deter you from attaining such blessings. But here's the kicker! This is where your faith needs to be amplified and this is where you need to trust the process and to keep going.

Everything you want is coming.

Relax. Let go. And watch God work.

God's plan is never straight forward.

Every betrayal, every heartache, every battle, every hardship you may face and every twist, turns, ups, and downs are all a part of his divine plan.

The magnitude of any problem you face is always relative to the size of your incoming blessing.

So keep the faith.

Trust him.

And remember; it's all a part of his plan.

Chapter Four

may you wear your strength like the grandest of diamonds.

Good For You

Your Physical Health Matters

A few years ago, I made a vow to myself to step out of my comfort zone and to explore more of the world.

I was living a very sheltered life that was narrated by my goals and dreams, directed by my passions and inadvertently executed by my need to be this accomplished woman whose aim is to break glass ceilings, build her own doors, and make herstory.

Now don't get me wrong, I am still that woman, but somewhere along the line, I was merely existing and not LIVING.

A few years back, I decided to (metaphorically) remove the shackles I had placed on myself, walk to the edge of my innermost fears, and jump.

Did I fall?

No, my darling. I gained wings I never thought I had, and I flew.

And—

I have been soaring ever since!

Xoxo

Your strength isn't defined by how much pain you can endure and carry, but instead by what you choose to put down and walk away from.

It's important to do a quick self-check on your mental state. Ask yourself questions like: am I feeling down? Am I feeling anxious? Have I made any significant behavioural changes recently? If you can answer 'yes' to these questions, it might be time to find a little help to make sure your mental health is in tip-top shape.

Being too active or not active enough can both lead to poor mental health. If, at any time you are feeling overwhelmed, don't be afraid to say 'enough is enough.' Stay active, but take breaks when you need them.

Your pain gives birth to your purpose. Nurture yourself during your most challenging times.

While it's fine to have friends on social media, nothing can replace face-to-face contact. We all need real and substantial relationships with loved ones. Cultivate having real connections in your life.

When was the last time you cried? I know you may have been brainwashed into thinking that crying is a sign of weakness, but that's a far cry (pun intended) from the truth. Crying releases oxytocin and endorphins. These chemicals make you feel good and may also ease both physical and emotional pain. Crying also regulates your emotions, gives you a sense of calmness, reduces distress, and promotes a sense of well-being. So cry, baby girl. Cry and let it all out.

Laughter is the best medicine. It truly is. Like crying, laughter also triggers the release of endorphins, which promote an overall sense of well-being. It's good for your mood, your mental health, your heart health, and more. Do you need another reason to LOL right now? Before you read the next mindful practice, give yourself a big 'ole laugh and add it to your self-care to-do list!

Remember; to take lots of pictures and keep a journal... for in the long run, they will keep you.

Remember that expensive perfume or fancy dress you have been saving for the perfect time? Now is the perfect time. Put it on today and dress up for no reason.

If you continuously bend yourself backwards for others or continue to pour and give, you'll leave yourself empty and depleted.

One of the most crucial parts of self-care is ignoring those who are committed to misunderstanding you. Nothing gets people more upset than when they realize that they no longer control you or that you are no longer giving them your power.

In these unprecedented and revolutionary times, ask yourself this: do I have the capacity for this?

Prioritize getting quality sleep. Sleep deprivation is the root cause of most diseases.

Stress is the number one killer above all else. Find ways to ground yourself; that way, when life throws you lemons you can faithfully make lemonade.

Remember: the power to heal lies within you. Tap into your inner Goddess.

Be kind to yourself and be gentle with yourself.

Practice gratitude and meditate daily.

Travel alone….at least once in your life. For in order for us women to grow internally and externally we need real moments of solitude and self-reflection to balance out just how much of ourselves we give away.

Fall in love with yourself over and over and over again.

Chapter Five

may you always remember who you are.

Good For You

You Matter

Stacy-Ann Buchanan

When I was going through my divorce, I questioned everything about who I was as a woman.

I questioned my natural independence.
I questioned my drive to succeed.
I questioned my quest to set yearly, monthly, and quarterly goals.
I questioned my wants to secure financial bags.
I questioned my need for constant growth- emotionally and mentally.

I basically questioned my strength.

This strength that I had acquired from being raised by my Father.

One day—with tears welled up in my eyes—I went to my father's house and asked him: WHY?? Why did he raised me to be so strong, so independent—to raise my hand and standards every chance I got, to ask uncomfortable questions, to have a voice, to take up space, to secure my financial freedom, to run with the wind, to talk back when I felt silenced, to build my own doors. I said, "Daddy, you raised me to have all these attributes, but the one thing you forgot to do was to raise me to be a wife."

Without questioning me as to why I felt like this or where this was coming from, my Dad looked me straight into my eyes and said, "I raised you to be a somebody, not somebody's. Remember that."
....and with those words, I remembered who I was. I put my crown back on and I made one of the best decisions of my life—I left a mediocre life and started to live my best life ever!

xoxo

Big up yuh BLOODCLAAT self!

The most powerful thing you can do as a woman is own your narrative (the good, bad, and the ugly). Unapologetically own it all—that's the spreadsheet for a peaceful life.

Self-confidence is the best outfit a woman can wear. Rock it and own it!

Gift yourself the experience of LUXURY:
Living
Unlimited
Xtraaaa-ness
(with)
Unequivocal
Relaxation
(and loving of)
Yourself.

If you want to achieve greatness, stop asking for permission.

Go out there and take up space, be your authentic self, celebrate yourself, be kind to yourself, appreciate your journey, don't play the comparison game and more importantly, know that queen lies inside you.

Nuh mek no baddy tek yuh fi eediat. Translation – don't let anyone play you for a fool.

Normalize celebrating your wins.

When they call you aggressive or bitchy, keep on being assertive.
When they call you bossy, keep on leading.
When they call you difficult, keep on speaking and walking in your truth.
When they call you too much, keep on taking up space and letting your light shine.
When they call you awkward, keep on asking tough questions.
When they call you high-maintenance, keep on knowing your worth and do not settle for less.
At the end of the day it doesn't matter what you do—you'll forever be criticized. But you'll save a lot of time by not worrying too much about what other people think about you. The earlier in your life that you can learn that, the easier the rest of it will be.

It's a pivotal moment in life when you meet these two kind of women:

1. The woman who can break several times and puts herself together again using nothing but self-love.
2. The woman who knows her strength isn't determined by what she chooses to carry, but rather what she chooses to put down.

Look around you: are you still standing after all that you've been through? Have you taken the time to invest in therapy or follow more therapists on social media? Have you made a conscious decision to break generational trauma? Are you on your healing journey? If yes, then you—my love—are one powerful Goddess.

Whenever you feel discouraged, remind yourself that you're here for a defined purpose and that you can do anything you set your mind to.

The need for approval from others kills your freedom.

The desire to get people to like you and to love what you do is fuelled by anxiety. That will then create a fence of fear that subconsciously blocks you from realizing the depths of your own worth and the greatness that's within you.

When you rid yourself of the need to always feel accepted, liked, or even loved, you create a space for self-love, self-care and self-appreciation. Adapt this concept and watch your confidence level go from 'I hope they like me' to 'I'm fabulous either way!'

Right now, ask yourself: do I need their approval?

Visualize yourself in the position/life that you want, and start moving accordingly.

Nobody glows brighter than the woman who knows her worth, practices gratitude, and loves the f___ outta herself.

Know that you are purposely and divinely crafted and designed by God. Every inch of you is a manifestation of his love. You are the personification of magic. Don't let a mofo try you!

External validation isn't necessarily a bad thing....
However, it becomes unhealthy when you depend on it so much that your life and your actions are guided by external approval.
Relying on external validation can make you anxious or depressed.
Remember: people's opinions are just that—their opinions. They shouldn't make or break you.

Please stop putting so much stock into what other people think.

You got this. Stay true to you. Clap for your damn self. And remember, as long as you validate you, you'll be alright!
(note to self)

How you 'gon let Suzette make you reverse your growth?
How you 'gon let Peter drag you back to a place you dug yourself out of?
How you 'gon let Chad redefine you?
Listen. Stop.
We all know growth is a powerful drug.
We all know healing one's self is a revolution.
So what you not 'gon do is let anybody take you back to a level you, yourself levelled up from.
Okay?
Thank you.

Good For You

Don't think you deserve the job?
Apply for it anyways.
Don't think your article is good enough?
Publish it anyway.
Don't think they'll reply to your email?
Send it anyways.
Listen. You ain't self-rejecting no more!

*Repeat this to yourself daily:
'I didn't come this far, to only come this far!'*

Raise your standards—emotionally, physically, spiritually, and financially— then add revenue recognition tax.

Stacy-Ann Buchanan

Date the heck outta yourself!

Drink a glass of 'confidence champagne' every day. Bathe yourself in self-love. Stroll on your personal red carpet of self-appreciation. Wear your vulnerability like the grandest of diamonds. Fly in the private jet of your purpose. Secure your bags without any announcements. Drink your cucumber-infused water. Mind your business. Practice gratitude. Pray daily. And lastly, remind yourself that you're loved, that you are evolving, and that your batty is getting rounder!

Speak the language of gratitude.
Manifest your dreams.
Walk by faith and not by sight.
And always, always rebuke the
bare minimum.

Manifest multiple streams of income and multiple streams of peace.

Put yourself on your priority list.

The more you choose you, the more you will be drawn to others who do the same. Starting NOW—choose yourself!!

In everything that you do, always remember, you—well, we got this!!!

Good For You

.... the end

Thank you for allowing me to share my thoughts and mindful practices with you.

This book is a long time coming, but I wanted to make sure that the space I carved out to share these were met with a plethora of options that you can relate to and adapt to your growth.

During the darkest times of my life—when I battled depression and suicidal ideations—I wrote letters to my future self as means of staying afloat and staying alive. These letters helped me to move past the pain and hurt I was experiencing and to focus on the trajectory of my survival and healing.

The simple act of writing and journaling my thoughts, aspirations and wishes proved to be an essential tool that helped me fight the battles of staying alive.

Years ago, I read a quote that says: "Every woman should keep a journal, because in the end, it will keep her." My oh my, how true that statement turned out to be. The letters that I wrote to my future self truly kept me. Reading them back was and still is a beautiful reminder that in midst of uncertainty, my faith was a lot stronger than I was and that my pain birthed my purpose. For that I am grateful.

Before I end this book, I wanted to leave space for you to do this exercise.

When you have the capacity, when you're free from distractions, when you find a peaceful moment....use these last pages to write a letter to your future self: healed, complete, confident and lacking nothing. Let her know you are proud of her, that she's seen, she is loved and she is all sorts of—yasses!

Your future self will thank you for it.

XOXO

Good For You

Date:

Dear Future _____ ,

About The Author

Buchanan's impact, entrepreneurial work ethic and achievements have led her to being selected as one of the 100 Black Women to Watch in Canada, one of the 150 Black Women Making Canada Better, one of the 150 Leading Canadians for Mental Health and landing a TEDx Talk. The self-directed and self-funded award winning documentary, The Blind Stigma, made Canadian history when it debuted as the first documentary produced in Canada that takes an in-depth look at how mental health is perceived within the Black community, and cemented Buchanan as a documentary filmmaker. As a recognized brand, The Blind Stigma has since branched out into a podcast that continues to explore such stigmas, dissect the multiple factors that aid towards mental illness in Black communities and provides a safe space for stories to be heard. Her body of work has firmly planted her career on disrupting systemic anti-Black racism by taking holistic approaches to dismantle the stigmas of how mental health is constructed and perceived.

Through raising awareness, directing positive dialogues to fuel resources, and orchestrating safe, transformative spaces for Black voices to be amplified, Stacy-Ann Buchanan's ultimate objective is to take back the Black narrative.

ps: may you always know what you need, for you to be you.

www.ingramcontent.com/pod-product-compliance
Lightning Source LLC
Chambersburg PA
CBHW071346080526
44587CB00017B/2993